Gain unprecedented clarity and direction.

"Being a hero" is the core mindset that will reveal your true purpose in life, how you best create value for others, and the specific audience you want to be a hero to. Gain the clarity and direction you need with one simple question.

Being A Hero Is About Them

It's About *Their* Bigger Future

Transforming Their D.O.S.

They Grow, You Expand

Your Crucial Contribution

Easy To Commit For 25 Years

Heroes Attract Each Other

Exponential Hero Networks

Six Ways To Enjoy This Strategic Coach Book

Text **60 Minutes**	The length of our small books is based on the time in the air of a flight between Toronto and Chicago. Start reading as you take off and finish the book by the time you land. Just the right length for the 21st-century reader.
Cartoons **30 Minutes**	You can also gain a complete overview of the ideas in this book by looking at the cartoons and reading the captions. We find the cartoons have made our Strategic Coach concepts accessible to readers as young as eight years old.
Audio **120 Minutes**	The audio recording that accompanies this book is not just a recitation of the printed words but an in-depth commentary that expands each chapter's mindset into new dimensions. Download the audio at **strategiccoach.com/go/hero**
Video **30 Minutes**	Our video interviews about the concepts in the book deepen your understanding of the mindsets. If you combine text, cartoons, audio, and video, your understanding of the ideas will be 10x greater than you would gain from reading only. Watch the videos at **strategiccoach.com/go/hero**
Scorecard **10 Minutes**	Go to the Mindset Scorecard at the end of this book to score your "hero" mindset. First, score yourself on where you are now, and then fill in where you want to be a year from now. Download additional copies at **strategiccoach.com/go/hero**
ebook **1 Minute**	After absorbing the fundamental ideas of the concept of being a hero, you can quickly and easily share them by sending the ebook version to as many other individuals as you desire. Direct them to **strategiccoach.com/go/hero**

Thanks to the Creative Team:

Adam Morrison

Kerri Morrison

Hamish MacDonald

Shannon Waller

Jennifer Bhatthal

Victor Lam

Margaux Yiu

Christine Nishino

Willard Bond

Peggy Lam

Who Do You Want To Be A Hero To?

Not all heroes wear capes. You might not think of yourself as a hero, but every time you create value for others, you're benefiting people and making life easier or better for them in some way.

The question is, "Who do you want to be a hero to?" By identifying the key audience you want to create value for, you focus yourself on the most crucial people in your life, helping them to grow their capabilities—and growing your own as well.

Cartoons by Hamish MacDonald.

Printed in Toronto, Canada. The Strategic Coach Inc., 33 Fraser Avenue, Suite 201, Toronto, Ontario, M6K 3J9.

This publication is meant to strengthen your common sense, not to substitute for it. It is also not a substitute for the advice of your doctor, lawyer, accountant, or any of your advisors, personal or professional.

If you would like further information about The Strategic Coach® Program or other Strategic Coach® services and products, please telephone 416.531.7399 or 1.800.387.3206.

Library of Congress Control Number: 2019910734
Author Academy Elite, Powell, OH 43065

Available via Audiobook and:
Print: 978-1-64085-806-0
Ebook: 978-1-64085-808-4

Contents

Introduction
Everybody Loves A Hero
You recognize that your two greatest kinds of experiences in life are someone being a hero to you and your being a hero to someone else.

In my many conversations with people about the greatest experiences of their professional and personal lives, a recurring theme emerges: They tell me about a time when someone was a hero to them.

These experiences always make them feel incredibly positive about that person, and that positivity is permanent— even decades later, the memory of it is vivid.

The other experience that constantly shows up as a great one for people is having the opportunity to be a hero to someone else.

By "being a hero," I don't mean that you have to leap off a cliff for somebody. It can be as simple as connecting two people who would have a great business partnership. There are situations that come up where your intention is to help another person just for the purpose of helping them—that's what I mean by being a hero.

Best outside reality.
We do a lot of funny thinking about what's real and what isn't because there often seem to be discrepancies between what's happening inside of ourselves and what's happening outside of ourselves.

So what can you use as a constant outside reference point to check out the reality of who you are, and in such a way that you don't have to give too much thought to it?

Here's the answer: your measurable impact on other people's growth and achievement. It continually proves the reality of your own unique progress, and that's one attractive part of the idea of growing yourself as a hero to an increasing number of other individuals.

It's measurable quantitatively because their progress is being measured, but it's also qualitative because the people you're a hero to give you feedback on how your help was crucial to their growth.

It's all related to specifics: a specific individual, specific progress and results, and the specific capability or set of capabilities you bring to the process.

When it's someone else.
The best way to determine how you can be a hero to someone is by considering the times that other people have uniquely contributed to your own success in being a more capable and confident individual.

As you increasingly become a hero to other people, you become more keenly aware of how other people are being heroes to you.

It expands in both ways, and the deep appreciation you feel when someone else is a hero to you is what other people feel when you're a hero to them.

But if you're always giving without taking, or you're always taking without giving back, the benefits will run dry. The reality has to increase both inside of yourself and outside of yourself—they're necessary for each other.

When you're the hero.

If you think back, you'll probably find you're most proud of all the times and situations when your performance and contribution enabled others to grow and achieve in ways that were crucially important for them.

And it's never about what you think the other person should do; it's about what they really want to do and see as being crucial for themselves.

Just as you're always working toward a future you envision, when you're a hero to someone else, you're operating with their version of the future in mind. It's important to be helpful based on the other person's purpose, and help in a way that's in accordance with their own game plan.

Instant powerful focus.

Being a hero is always the purpose that most focuses and multiplies our best energies and skills in any situation.

It's like having a constant true north—you've established the correct direction right from the beginning, and you're not worried about the means because the means will be whatever's necessary to get there.

There's no way to predict exactly what means will be required, but being a hero to other people can always be the focus of your own development of capability. That's the direction you can always be going in.

With so many people you could spend your time helping, deciding who it is you want to be a hero to can take away all complexity from the situation by eliminating the alternatives and setting you up to move ahead with a clear goal and purpose.

The question, "Who do you want to be a hero to?" helps you narrow down and define your purpose in life by identifying your true audience and how you can create value for them.

Nothing's appreciated more.

No matter who we are or where we are, we deeply appreciate everyone who's ever been a hero to us, and every one of those people has the same deep appreciation for every person who's been a hero to them.

This is a constant reality, and it can be a focusing purpose for you as it is for many others.

All of this intense meaning, purpose, and value creation starts with just this one thing: someone contributing crucially to another individual's growth and achievement.

And it works best when the only reason you're doing it is because you can be crucially useful to another person.

It doesn't matter who you are or where you are. Getting clear about who you want to be a hero to tells you about what capabilities you need to focus on and what capabilities of others you need to surround yourself with so you can keep expanding.

From a single individual to teamwork, you can have your whole organization being a hero to the right audience.

Chapter 1
Being A Hero Is About Them

You're amazed at how being a hero to someone else always expands your awareness, capabilities, and value outward in the world.

I know a lot of people who have big, world-affecting ideas, but the world is general, not specific, and no one truly has an experience with the entire world.

You might guess that the famous giants of technology who have affected the world think globally, but I bet if you asked them who is actually meaningful to them, it would come down to about the same number of people that are meaningful to you.

And that's your world: the specific individuals you can be a hero to and who are heroes to you.

Useful outside of yourself.

Every time you do something uniquely useful for someone else, who you are becomes clearer to you.

You can't figure out how you can be useful to others if you stay in your own little bubble, because how you can be useful is relative to the people you want to be useful to, who you want to be a hero to.

You have to see how your unique capabilities fit in with what they're trying to achieve for themselves and their future.

And the more you figure out how you can be useful to someone else, the smarter you'll get at figuring it out in new situations.

Making them more capable.

You can use your capabilities to guide and support others to grow their own capabilities in ways that are uniquely important for them.

Other people becoming more capable is the way that you can measure your usefulness outside of yourself. That's the real measurement—that as a result of knowing you, they become more capable.

Trying to measure your usefulness from inside of yourself— having thoughts like, "I'm so valuable and so useful, and I should be recognized for my usefulness"—is strictly hallucinatory, because you can't check out what effect you're having unless you actually go outside of yourself. Until you test it outside yourself, it's just an abstraction.

It's best done with an individual you know, and you can discuss it with them and get feedback from them. You get a constant feedback loop between the two of you as you become more capable.

Escaping from "the me trap."

Your growing power of being a hero to an increasing number of people outside of yourself will free you completely from the isolating and confusing self-centeredness that seems to trap so many others in today's world.

I've noticed more and more that our culture is all about "me, me, me." When I was growing up, the world had been through the Great Depression and the Second World War, and it was all about people being heroes.

The public discourse was about what people had sacrificed and contributed.

There's a big difference between what I see currently and what I experienced in my teen years. When I was growing up, the whole notion that your job was supposed to make you happy and that you're supposed to love your work was an unknown thought because during the Great Depression, just having a job of any kind was a crucial thing. And the war veterans who survived and came back just wanted to get back to a normal life.

The possibilities for individuals have expanded a great deal over the past 50 years.

At Strategic Coach, we only want our team members to be doing the work they love doing, and this is because we don't want anything to interfere with their ability to be heroes to one another and to our clients.

No status, no comparison.

You can now have the secure sense that being a hero is a permanent daily source of new capabilities and confidence that increasingly eliminates any need for you to worry about your status or to compare your experience with any other person's lifetime success.

You're unique, so no comparison is even possible. The only question is, do you come to grips with your own uniqueness and use it to make yourself more useful to other people?

Negative issues around status and comparison only come into play when you don't know what it is you're uniquely good at and how you can be really useful.

The uniqueness of what you do can't be proven inside of yourself; it can only be proven by its impact on the world outside of you.

And the best way to have an impact outside of yourself is to help other people become more capable.

The proof of your capability is that other people become more capable as a result of interacting with you.

Endless reciprocal learning.
Your best learning in all areas of life doesn't come from "you" or from "them," but rather from the extraordinarily unpredictable creative energy generated every time you're being a hero to another person.

Your being a hero to someone and that person being a hero to you can be a constant, and each of you creates a reality out of being a hero, even though the circumstances in which you're operating are always changing.

You can create opportunities for being a hero to someone out of changing circumstances because you'll suddenly discover that these can be newly used and newly focused.

This is how you'll constantly find surprising new ways to be a hero to someone, just as other people are finding surprising new ways to be a hero to you, and how you'll keep getting more capable no matter what happens in the world.

THE "ME" TRAP
HOW DO I EVEN KNOW I'M REAL?!
IS ANYONE ELSE REAL?
I FEEL SO ALONE!
WHAT DOES IT ALL MEAN?!
NOBODY VALUES ME!
IT'S NOT ABOUT YOU...

Chapter 2
It's About *Their* Bigger Future

You gain great clarity and confidence from knowing that enabling other people's improvement and growth uniquely accelerates your own.

When you're given compliments, which is likely to happen when you're providing a unique capability that helps move someone toward achieving their goals and the future they want, remember this: if it's the right audience, the audience is always right.

If they tell you that you're crucially important, then you are.

To deny or to not accept those complimentary comments is to do violence to reality.

If you don't accept the other person's feedback, you're undermining the value you created for them, and you're undermining your own capability to do it again.

If they accept your contribution but you don't accept their compliment, then you've broken the loop, the energy flow between the two of you, by showing that you don't care and that it isn't about them for you. Accepting complimentary feedback graciously is an important part of being a hero to someone.

Freedom from "unfairness."
When you focus on being more of a hero to other people, it instantly and automatically eliminates all thoughts about the world, or life, being unfair to you.

Fairness isn't a factor. It isn't about fairness—it's about usefulness.

The world wasn't designed for you. If there are times when it seems like it was, chalk that up to coincidence. We're born into reality, but what makes our reality truly real is going outside of ourselves and having a useful impact there.

We can make the world more and more designed for us, but only as a byproduct of being useful to others. When we're focused on fairness, we're focused on ourselves. When we're focused on value creation, we're focused on others.

If you're stuck in a discussion about unfairness, it means you're a spectator, not a player. If you want things to be more "fair," be more useful. The people you're a hero to will not only treat you fairly, they'll treat you as uniquely crucial.

No more self-stagnation.

Every measurable improvement you help other people make in their lives also has the immediate impact of releasing you from situations in your own life where you've felt stagnant and stuck.

There's no leverage inside of your own world that you can use to get yourself unstuck. The place you'll find the leverage is outside of yourself.

For example, I had spent years thinking that Strategic Coach should be producing videos, but I found that I just couldn't get myself to start doing them.

Then we started a project that involved doing videos for someone else. I watched the whole process, seeing what worked and what didn't work. Within three months of completing that project, after having not acted on doing videos for ten years, we immediately had a video studio, and I was pumping out videos.

The only reason I could do videos for myself was because we developed that capability in order to create value for someone else.

Catching up in one jump.

This whole new focus of being a hero in other people's lives will make you feel that you're taking a huge jump in terms of your own future—that in any area you've felt that you're falling behind, you instantly start making the best possible progress.

The experience of being useful is a complete experience no matter where you start. Even the first time you do it, it's 100 percent. You're doing all of what you can do.

The only question is, do you want to have more of that experience?

Being clear on who you want to be a hero to is a big part of the jump. You cut away all the other distractions and immediately know exactly what to focus on and how you can contribute uniquely to progress being made in that person's life.

Multiplying from the outside in.

You're going to become increasingly observant about and skillful at learning from how your *external* assistance to other individuals to achieve their bigger and better future can almost immediately propel your own *internal* improvements.

If you do something for someone else's sake, there's an immediate reward that you get from that: you now have the capability you developed in order to help them for yourself. And you can then also share that capability with others for whom it's relevant. If you've paid attention and refined something so that it works for one person, you can be assured that it will work for other people as well.

Things really do come to people who look for opportunities they can help with and take action on it.

Always becoming more useful.

You can continually develop, deepen, and expand every-thing that makes you more useful in the lives and futures of those individuals who are most important to you, always making you into a bigger and better hero to them.

It's difficult for a lot of people to get and be comfortable with only being a hero to people who are important to them. I've been asked, "But what about all the other people who aren't as important to me?"

Those other people will be important to someone else, but you aren't responsible for them.

You can't think of things in a general way, in terms of helping all of humanity, because humanity isn't a substitute for actual individuals.

You're responsible for being useful to the people who are important to you.

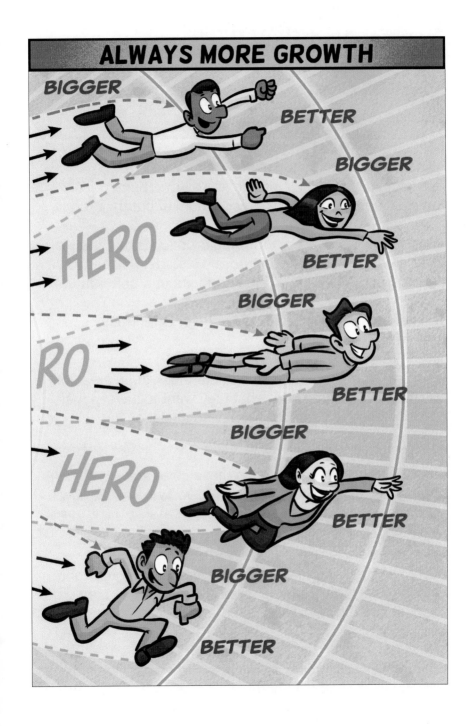

Chapter 3
Transforming Their D.O.S.

You're certain that being a hero starts by first understanding other individuals' biggest dangers, opportunities, and strengths.

All heroism you engage in takes place within your relationships with other people and allows them to feel more excited, motivated, and confident about their future.

What we've discovered at Strategic Coach is that there are three areas that are the best possible starting places for getting people to entertain thoughts about a better future.

The acronym for it is D.O.S.—Dangers, Opportunities, and Strengths.

If you ask someone questions about those three areas of life, they will let you know what they want to have in their future—if they're interested in having a relationship with you at all.

If you can engage with them in these three areas, you can begin a discussion that will reveal to you where and how you can be a hero to them.

Where everybody's future starts.

Every human being makes unique personal progress only by continually transforming three specific factors they encounter in their lives at all times: dangers, opportunities, and strengths.

What makes something a danger is the possibility of losing something. It can be something we already have that we could lose, or it could be something that's possible but we'll lose the possibility if we don't take action on it.

Opportunity is the possibility of a gain, and we can feel opportunity in all of the same places we can feel danger. These are the exciting areas we want to maximize and capture.

Strengths are what we become suddenly aware of and clear about regarding our existing resources and capabilities. They give us confidence when we're up against a danger as well as when we're confronted with an opportunity.

D — Sudden simplicity and clarity.

Something that you're striving for when being a hero to someone is to get them away from being embroiled in a lot of confusing experiences and reactions.

There's a part of their brain that can simplify and clarify things, and the best way to bring that simplicity and clarity into their thinking is with a question.

Simply by asking, "What are your three biggest dangers that need to be eliminated?" you're immediately triggering the possibility of sudden clarity and confidence in another person's picture of their future.

By being clear about our dangers, we have everything we need to move toward a solution to them. Thinking about things in general terms—for instance, "Nothing's working"—can have a paralyzing effect. But when you list only the biggest things that are in your way, you have what to focus on.

The next step is to put a date on it by asking what they'd

like to have eliminated from their lives three months from now. By doing this, you're letting them engage with the idea of getting rid of what's bothering them. But you're not necessarily the one who's solving the problem here. You're allowing them to be the person to solve their own problem.

O — Next extraordinary jump.

Once you have the foundation of clarity and confidence, the next question to ask is, "What are the three biggest opportunities you need to capture?"

This causes the individual you're helping to immediately become extraordinarily engaged with and committed to their next biggest jump in achievement. After giving them relief from the possibility of a loss by identifying their biggest dangers, you've immediately moved on to the possibility of a big gain.

Of course, someone might be faced with more than three dangers and three opportunities at any given time, but prioritizing and focusing on engaging with the biggest three will allow the person to realize they can deal with all of them and to see how they can do it.

S — Maximizing their strengths.

Your achievement as a hero is always permanently sealed in place by asking the individual you're helping a third question: "What are the three most important strengths you already have that you can immediately use to transform your biggest dangers and opportunities?"

When you're facing eliminating the possibility of loss and capturing the possibility of gain, every single relevant and specific strength that's useful to the situation is brought to bear.

These three questions work because you don't and can't know the answers to any of them. Only the person you're asking knows the answers. There can't be any self-interest on your part. It's all about the other person achieving simplicity and clarity, feeling the possibility of an extraordinary jump, and suddenly maximizing their strengths.

This is all internal to them. You've created a space in which help from the outside has allowed them to transform themselves on the inside. That's where all heroism starts.

Your guaranteed hero territory.

If you're excited about this possibility of being a hero, know that you can always do it through these three questions geared to different parts of another person's experience as they visualize their future.

From now until the end of your life, every time you help specific individuals to transform their unique D.O.S. factors into bigger and better results, you're being a hero.

Even if you ask the three questions and discover that you don't possess any of the required capabilities to move the person toward their goal, and instead point them toward another outside resource and capability, you've still done your job and are being a hero to them.

You can have all the skills in the world, but you won't be able to be useful to other people without an understanding of the D.O.S. formula, which helps you figure out what it is you can contribute for someone else's benefit.

Chapter 4
They Grow, You Expand
Your hero confidence continually increases because the more you help others grow, the more your capabilities to be a hero expand.

Each of us is alone inside our own brain.

The only time you're not alone is when your brain connects with someone else's—and the best possible connection you can make with another person's brain is to ask them about their future.

If you use the D.O.S. formula to ask them about their dangers, opportunities, and strengths, you're stacking the odds that it's either going to be the best possible start to a relationship, or else there's not going to be any start at all.

In both cases, you could consider it a positive thing, because you either used your time 100 percent fully by creating value for them, or you didn't waste any of your time pursuing something that was never going to go anywhere.

No greater knowledge is needed.
The knowledge you need to continually grow as a hero in other people's lives isn't contained in your brain but rather is created in other individuals' brains when you motivate their imaginations with your three D.O.S. questions.

You just have to know how to ask the questions, and a key aspect is that you're not included at all in the questions. A lot of people go through their entire lives without asking a question that isn't about them, but it's impossible to be self-centered *and* be a hero to somebody else.

To be a hero, you have to want to be useful, and your own knowledge and experiences won't come into play until you've heard the other person's answers to your questions about their future.

The first time you ask the D.O.S. questions will be the scariest, because it will be entirely new territory for you, and most likely also for the person you're asking the questions.

But after some repetition, asking the three questions will start to feel natural, like anything else you've learned to talk about.

Doesn't matter where or when.

The reason there isn't more heroism in the world is that the burdens of constantly reacting to what's going on outside of ourselves often prevents us from granting other people space in which we're totally listening to them while they're talking about themselves.

When you're being a hero, on the other hand, you're completely agreeable up front that what they say about their future doesn't have anything to do with you.

You now know that when you give someone else that space, and give them that time that's entirely about them and not you, you benefit by becoming uniquely useful and a hero to them.

After you learn about how they see their future by listening to their answers to the D.O.S. questions, it will immediately become clear to you what capabilities and resources you have that can help them.

All of your best future opportunities to be a continually greater hero lie entirely in your helping others to endlessly expand their abilities to transform their most important D.O.S. issues.

Abundant possibilities all around.
All of the situations and circumstances you'll ever need to always become an even bigger and better hero are immediately available to you in the relationships you already have, which will connect you to an increasing number of others.

There are always opportunities to engage in being a hero to someone, as everyone is experiencing dangers, opportunities, and strengths at all times.

All you have to do, no matter what kind of mood you're in or what might be on your mind regarding your own future, is to take the focus off of yourself for that period of time and allow the focus to be entirely on the other person as you use the D.O.S. formula.

You can make that shift from being self-centered to being a hero instantaneously.

And once you get good at being a hero to someone, you're going to become choosy about who you do it for, taking into account what would be best for your own future growth and that of your company.

The word will go around.
It might be that, by reading this book, you'll know more about being a hero than anyone else you know—and those individuals you're a hero to will quickly spread the word

about your unique value to others.

The experience of having someone else's attention be entirely on them is so rare that people will naturally want to talk about it. After all, if you have an amazing conversation, the likes of which you've never experienced before, you're going to want to tell people about it.

While most people's main concern might be making themselves interesting, people will recognize your unique value because of your focus on being *interested*.

Don't waste your time trying to be a hero to people who don't want someone to be a hero to them. If this is the case, it will become clear to you when you're asking the D.O.S. questions—they'll refuse to answer.

But as you become a hero to receptive people, you'll become more and more referable.

The activity grows itself.
You'll discover that every time you're a hero to someone, it's an achievement, outcome, and overall experience you'll want to do over and over again at every opportunity.

It's like a drug, but one that's entirely positive for everyone involved.

As you do this, great things happen to you—you grow in the best possible way as you're being the most useful and doing the most good for other people.

You grow even though the spotlight is not on you.

Chapter 5
Your Crucial Contribution

You increasingly use your best capabilities to uniquely help certain individuals achieve goals that are crucial to their future growth.

As you grow your capability of being a hero, you become more particular about who you do it for.

Your time is valuable, and you know that when you're being a hero, the capabilities you bring to the table are unique and important.

When you contribute something, what you've done has an independent reality and a usefulness independent of the fact that you happened to do it.

Capabilities keep improving.

Because the impact of your being a hero has an independent reality apart from you, the contribution you make is measurable—even to people who aren't the recipients of your value creation. The impact is objective.

And it's not that you do it once and that's it. Having the intention and a process for using your time and capabilities to help others achieve their bigger and better goals automatically develops and expands your own capabilities.

You learn, make a bigger contribution, learn from that, make an even bigger contribution—it's an endless growth cycle in which you become more and more capable.

Totally unconventional.

This perspective of being a hero is not typical. Nobody

starts off being a hero, that's for certain—babies are the supreme egotists, focused exclusively on their own needs. Awareness of what's happening for others doesn't come until later, if at all!

Countless individuals today are anxiously and obsessively fixated on thinking about their own future. If, instead, you're focused on contributing to other people's futures, you've immediately bypassed a vast amount of conventional activity in the world around you.

No matter how good things are in society, everyone will have their own unique struggles. When you can see that someone important to you is struggling, you have a chance to become a hero to them.

How? By recognizing what you can do to help them achieve the future goals they care about most and by providing them with direction, confidence, and capability.

It might be easier to show up as a hero in bad times than good times, but when someone is spotlighted for being a hero in bad times, you'll probably find that they had a history of being a hero in good times too. They'd trained themselves to be a hero.

What no school ever taught you.
As you keep growing as a hero to others, you'll realize that you're in unique territory because none of the education and training you've had in your life ever pointed out and focused on the possibility of being a hero to others.

Even going through school in the particular historical period

41

when I did, when certain social customs and consciousness of others were very much the accepted way of things, the education system was all about being "normal." When you finished your education, there was a job in a factory or an office out there just waiting for you to fit yourself into it.

There was never any mention whatsoever about being a hero.

And this is even more true with education today, where the predominant narrative is about how unfair the world is and how everything's falling apart. The exception to this is those few great teachers who are heroes to their students by being focused on developing their unique potential.

Rewards keep getting bigger.

You're going to discover that this whole process of being a hero automatically and increasingly rewards you— without your even having to concern yourself with how it's happening.

That's because being a hero always makes use of you in the best possible way. And you get massive new opportunity to be great when you're operating at your best.

You get a deepening and an expansion of the capability that makes you a hero out in the world, and you become more of who you are at your most important.

I'm a competent writer and a competent artist, but when I'm helping somebody, I never offer them my writing skills or my artistic skills. I offer them my capability of asking questions they've never heard before, because I've learned I'm at my best when I'm using that skill.

I offer them what I'm uniquely good at because working in that zone dramatically increases the chance that I'm going to be a hero to them.

As you do this, you become more capable in the ways that are most unique to you and are also extraordinarily useful to other people.

Crucial "three times" formula.

Your personal future as a hero is now permanently simplified. It's always a matter of a single "three times" formula: your *crucial capabilities* focused on uniquely helping *crucial individuals* to achieve goals that are *crucial to their future growth*.

You're not making up your own importance here. The other person's goals and growth are real, as is the contribution you make to help them achieve those goals and growth.

We humans transform one another. The more people there are in the world, the more chances there are to be a hero—and the greater the quality of life is for the entire human population.

And with the three crucial elements in the "three times" formula—your capabilities, other individuals, and the other individuals' goals—it's exponential. It's not addition, it's a multiplier.

Chapter 6
Easy To Commit For 25 Years

You're increasingly relaxed by the growing certainty that being a unique hero in other people's futures can keep growing over the next 25 years.

You now know how to be a hero to other people—you know the three questions in the D.O.S. formula, and you can enable other individuals to answer those questions.

If committing to being a hero to certain people is something you want to do, you have to take into account that you have a limited amount of time, a limited amount of attention, and practical goals of your own to get to.

So an enormous part of being a hero to others is asking yourself who you want to be a hero to—because you can't be a hero to everybody.

What kind of person is the best person for you to be a hero to in your own life?

Go out 25 years and work backward.
You can now ask yourself the single most important question for the rest of your life: "Who do I want to be a hero to right now—and this would be even more exciting and fulfilling for me 25 years from now?"

Once you have an answer to that question clearly in mind, you can go ahead and design your life backward from the future.

The reason most people don't commit to things for a time period as long as 25 years is they're not heroes.

They can't guarantee their own behavior, they can't guarantee their own attention, and they can't guarantee that kind of commitment because what could possibly keep them fascinated and motivated for 25 years if it's not about them?

Keep refining your "exactly who."

There's a specific, special kind of person you can clearly visualize as who you want to be a hero to.

The moment you visualize someone who checks all of the boxes, you know this will always be more true as your capabilities to be an even bigger hero continue to grow with each specific achievement.

You have to keep evaluating who you want to be a hero to. It's not that this changes completely, but your standards go up. Your audience has to be a group that continually fascinates and motivates you.

It has to demand something of you that you don't already know. There has to be the possibility of growth to another level.

There might be people whom you'd want to ask the D.O.S. questions to and be a hero to right now, but you wouldn't get the same thing out of it in 25 years because you'll already have everything that you can gain from it by then.

100% yes — or not at all.

Out of the entire world population, there are specific kinds of individuals you could possibly want to be a bigger and better hero to for an entire 25-year period, and it's either totally affirmative or a complete zero.

What happens to a lot of entrepreneurs is that after some time, who they are and what their business is about is no longer heroic, and this is because their customers and clients aren't worth being heroes to in their minds.

It's been suggested that I take what Strategic Coach does into the school system, but I have no particular interest in being a hero to anyone there. That's not a setting that has any interest for me.

Nor do I want to be a hero to people in the corporate system, the government, or non-profit organizations. I'm one person, and there are 7.7 billion people on the planet. There's lots of room for other kinds of heroes.

100 quarters x passion and skill.

Knowing who you want to be a hero to means you can focus your greatest passion and most powerful skills for your next 100 quarters—the next 25 years of your life—and the only thing you need to focus on within this future framework is where you can best be a hero during the next 90 days.

The only thing you could possibly commit yourself to for 25 years would be something where you're guaranteed that you're going to be increasingly passionate and more skillful as you go along, and being a hero to people in the way we're talking about would definitely fit that bill.

And if you had the choice of either being a hero to someone for an hour or being more and more a hero to someone for 25 years, which would you choose?

You'd go the 25-year route because it clarifies your future.

The further into the future you can see the consequences of what you're doing, the more honest, ethical, and moral you'll be about doing it.

And while you can commit to 25 years knowing that it'll be better than ever by the time it ends, you only ever need to focus on what's available to you to do this quarter. After this one, you'll get another one.

Utilizing every new circumstance.
Your life will permanently simplify and clarify itself. Being a hero will now be your single most important daily focus and, therefore, the endless flow of new situations and circumstances over the next 25 years can all be engaged with and continually transformed with this hero focus in mind.

People are sometimes tempted to simplify their lives by withdrawing and disengaging, but this approach is the opposite: you're simplifying your life through deeper and deeper engagement with the world.

You're being fully present and alert, always ready to see how you can make a meaningful difference in someone's life by creating value for them in a way that only you can.

And this lifetime commitment will keep you fascinated, motivated, and constantly growing.

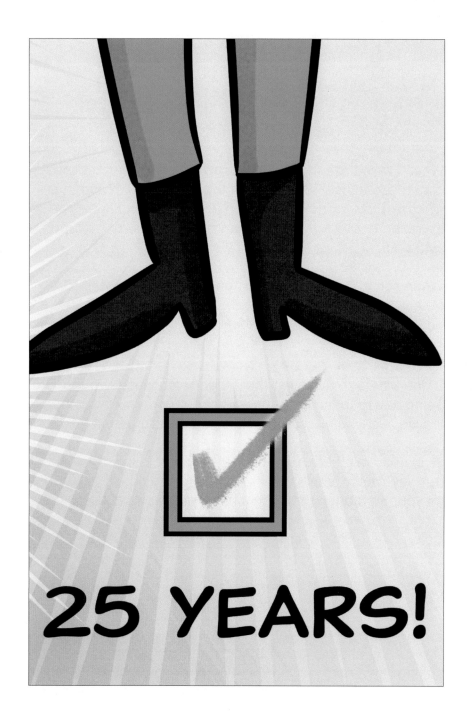

Chapter 7
Heroes Attract Each Other

You find that as you master being a crucial hero in others' lives, you also attract other heroes who will be creative collaborators with you.

When I recognize that someone else is also a hero, it immediately eliminates 90 percent of the uncertainty regarding whether I can work with them. If you're a hero, I know that it's going to be very easy to communicate and collaborate with you.

When someone's a hero, you know that not everything they do has to be strictly about themselves and their own future goals. They're focused on others.

Letting other heroes know.

Being a hero to even just one other person leads you to being a hero to an increasing number of others, and other individuals who are heroes will hear that you're one too.

When you're a hero to someone, they won't stay quiet about it—they'll appreciate it so much that they'll tell others, and so your reputation for being a hero will spread quickly.

Being a hero isn't a new thing. It's a particular way of looking at yourself in relationship to the world. There's an energetic quality to heroes that immediately notifies and identifies for you that that person is being a hero too.

Heroes can spot each other, and being a hero is an attractive quality to other heroes. Anytime we're being a hero—talking like a hero, acting like a hero, producing results like a hero—we're letting other people know who are also similarly motivated.

Normal way of living life.

Being a hero isn't something that's talked about or encouraged in normal daily life in the 21st century because most people think that it's something that can only happen in extraordinary circumstances, or in movies or novels.

We love that kind of entertainment because it's gripping, and it conjures up all sorts of thoughts about what it would be like for us to be in those situations. But there's no chance for most of us to practice being a hero in that sort of way in daily life.

The truth is that you don't need emergencies and disasters to have opportunities to be a hero. Being a hero is a way of looking at your relationships in everyday situations. It's about being fascinated and motivated to help someone else get to where they're trying to go.

People who actually are heroes in exceptional circumstances probably practiced being heroes in their daily lives before they found themselves in those situations.

Different in every way.

Being a hero by helping others to create bigger and better futures for themselves increasingly enables you to live a completely different life than those who are focused only on their own futures.

It seems that the default position for humans is to be obsessively focused on their own futures, but the entrepreneurs I've worked with who are heroes to their audiences function very differently.

They have an ability to suspend their own self-interest sufficiently to learn and understand someone else's future goals, and then to organize and create a growth opportunity for that other person where the entrepreneur's unique knowledge and skills are crucial to that other individual taking a jump to a higher level.

That ability to sufficiently suspend self-interest so that you can create massive value for other people is a tremendous skill and goes by many different names. I call it being a hero.

The idea of being a hero often conjures the image of saving someone in a life-or-death situation, but in our context, it's helping someone to have a bigger, better life.

Previously, heroism has been defined only on the level of *need*, but here, we're defining it on the level of *want*.

Because there's much more to life than just satisfying your needs.

Opposite of bureaucracy.
Wherever life is organized within bureaucratic structures and processes, being a hero is resisted, discouraged, and prevented because the whole purpose of bureaucracy is to systematically replace all need for individual heroism with predictable, collective procedures.

In bureaucracies—which include not only the government, but corporations and philanthropic organizations—the strategy for organizing human affairs continually develops so that no heroism is required.

It's not just that it's hard to be a hero in a bureaucracy; the whole purpose of the bureaucracy is to prevent it from happening.

What results is that some people become convinced they could never be a hero because they associate heroism only with what we see in movies and novels. They don't want to be compared to those heroes, and so they don't recognize the capability for heroism in themselves.

They don't want to live a life in which there are any exceptional circumstances. They want things to be predictable and calm.

Heroes collaborate with heroes.

If you keep increasing your individual capability to be a hero within the world of relationships you already have, every other hero who learns about you will find ways to collaborate with you.

All people who are heroes have a naturally attractive quality to other heroes, and you're able to spot one another.

In radio terms, it's like you hear either static or a clear station. Once you dial in to the hero band, you and all the other heroes are on the same band. You're connected.

Heroes inspire heroes, but no one can be forced to be a hero. Whether you want to tune in to that station is a decision that can only come from within.

Chapter 8
Exponential Hero Networks

You realize that the more you grow as a hero to certain individuals, the more you automatically connect with others who are doing the same.

It's impossible to keep heroism a secret.

Humans like to gossip, so you're being a hero to members of a species that will naturally want to tell other people about it. Think about it: if someone's being a hero to you, is your first instinct to keep it a secret?

The connection is automatic: other people who are also being heroes are going to hear about how you're being a hero.

It might not have been the same way in the past, but today, being a hero is a choice. If you're choosing to be a hero, it means you're sufficiently alert, curious, responsive, and resourceful, and you get to see things, notice things, and create things that you wouldn't get to do if you didn't have those qualities.

And you always have the choice of who it is that you're a hero to.

Always specific, never general.
Being a hero is always about transforming the future growth of specific individuals who are uniquely fascinating to you, and never about people in general.

I know people who love humanity, but they don't like individual humans.

Well, humanity doesn't have an email address. There's nothing you can do for humanity as a whole. Heroism at the level we're talking about has to be specific. It has to be for a particular individual in a particular situation.

The entryway to being a hero is always a relationship with one human being—with your having insight, awareness, and capabilities that you use so that another person can have a bigger and better future.

When you do this with one individual, you gain a wisdom about that particular type of individual, and you can then become a hero to more individuals of that type. For me, my focus has always been on entrepreneurs, and the more I'm a hero to them, the more I develop the skills to continue to be a hero to them.

Every human represents a complete universe of interesting things. When you try to deal with a multitude of people at once, you're staying on the surface. When you focus on an individual, you're much deeper.

Invisible to non-believers.
As you become a bigger and better hero, people who don't believe in heroism will never be able to see what you're doing, let alone understand it.

For a lot of entrepreneurs, if there isn't money, and there isn't ownership, then there isn't anything. For such people, being a hero has no place in how their world operates. It just doesn't correspond to how they see things.

Those are the people that you're invisible to. It's binary:

either someone can see your heroism 100 percent, or they can't see it at all.

The people who can recognize when you're being a hero are the people who are similarly motivated, people who use their own resources to help someone else grow because helping in that way is a highly enjoyable activity for them.

Life is happily not about you.

Here's a real test: how can you lead an increasingly enjoyable life and not have the focus be about you?

As your best capabilities make you more of a hero in other people's lives, you increasingly become happier without having to think about yourself.

There are all sorts of leisure activities that people take up when they reach a certain level of financial security, and none of those things interest me. What interests me is to take my abilities and make them available to certain other people so that they can make a jump to a higher level.

Life is about how I'm helping other people to grow and enjoy their lives.

The way in which you're a hero is unique to your particular skills and capabilities. And your uniqueness being valuable to other people has the result of making you very happy.

Heroes operate in networks.

From the moment you choose to be a hero to even just one other person, you immediately join a suddenly visible network of individuals who are choosing to do the same.

And the more you do it, the more clearly you'll see the network.

Nobody is the be-all and end-all hero to any one person; you're only supplying one thing for that individual, and they want lots of things.

What you do is pay attention to where the person's growth is headed, and consider whether there's more you can do for them.

Once you've entered the network and are surrounded by many other heroes, you can use those other heroes as resources to support the people you're being a hero to in the areas in which you don't personally have the unique skills and knowledge to help them.

You might not have the required capabilities to help someone overcome their obstacles and achieve their goals, but you can be a hero by connecting them to someone who does.

Faster, easier, bigger connections.
The endless growth process you've entered by being a hero increasingly and automatically connects you with other individuals whose unique hero capabilities continually expand your own.

Simply seeing how other people are heroes expands your notion of where you can go next. Imitation and repetition are still the two major ways in which human beings get better.

Just pay attention, and you'll see ways to do things that you've never seen before.

Conclusion
Lifetime Heroic Simplicity
You're energized and relaxed to realize that being a hero as a growing daily focus remarkably simplifies everything else that will be important to you for the rest of your life.

People often ask me, "How do you sort out your opportunities?"

I say, "Well, don't start there. Start with thinking about who it is that you want to be a hero to, and work backwards from there."

If you're considering whether you should take an opportunity, ask yourself whether it would help you increasingly be a hero to the people you want to be a hero to.

If the answer is "not really," it's best to pass on the opportunity. And if this is the case, you didn't really lose anything because there was nothing there for you in the first place; it didn't line up with your goal and focus of being a hero to specific individuals.

In this way, your being a hero can act as your true north on the compass, which is infinitely useful in a world of unlimited opportunities.

Just one kind of person.
You'll grow increasingly certain about the growing value you always want to provide to those specific people you want to be a hero to because you'll see that it transforms their results and your capabilities for the better.

Theoretically, you could be a hero to other people, but that would tire you out, whereas being useful to someone you want to be a hero to is energizing and only gets better the more you do it, with bigger results.

And the more experience you get in being a hero, the keener you're going to get regarding who you want to be a hero to.

You're going to only want to be in situations where the person you're being a hero to appreciates the value you're providing for them, while you appreciate the opportunity that being a hero to them provides.

It's a cross-appreciation, and it increases the value in your mind of what you're doing.

Unique you, unique them.

Your choice to be a hero will continually bring out the uniqueness of your most important knowledge and skills in ways that enable others to experience their own unique value.

When you make the choice to be a hero to someone else, what comes out of you are your unique capabilities. And when you provide your uniqueness to others, they get to identify their own uniqueness, and their uniqueness gets expanded.

Uniqueness multiplies uniqueness. And since the other person's unique capabilities grow, it expands their ability to be a hero themselves, because they'll put those unique capabilities to work in helping others to move toward their future goals.

Deepening and expanding.

You're going to find that you're always motivated to improve your hero capabilities by deepening your understanding of the unique individuals you want to help and by expanding the number of individuals whose futures you help to transform.

It's a natural tendency once you see that you can do something successfully with one person to want to see if you can do the same thing successfully with others.

But you'll naturally find that you do things differently with different people, and every time this happens, you'll learn new things that you can then transfer to new situations with new people. And you'll learn more and more about what makes you unique.

The currency of heroism is uniqueness. You're never going to bring your merely competent capabilities to being a hero. You'll bring only your unique ones, and so you'll always be providing the most value to your audience.

Authority on what they want.

By being consciously focused on understanding how specific individuals make progress in life, you'll naturally grow into being their best outside authority on what can be their next biggest and best growth jumps. Because you've studied them and the type of individual they are, you become the guide for the world they're operating in.

It's not that you necessarily know exactly what their next step should be, but you do know how it has to happen because you'll have seen it over and over again. Because of your experience, you'll have the map you can use to point out what direction to head in.

You'll be able to tell the person you're being a hero to, "Here's where you want to go, and here are the things you need to look out for."

Everything that grows them.
Your sense of personal capability and confidence is going to always be expanding every day for the rest of your life because you'll instinctively know more and more what the individuals you want to be a hero to require for their own increasing growth.

Since you're going to be a hero to these other unique individuals for the rest of your life, you're going to want to know every one of the different factors that need to be provided to them in order to give them clarity and direction.

You're going to want to always be on the lookout for short-cuts that allow those you're being a hero to to get where they're going faster, easier, and cheaper.

You'll find that you become passionate about anything that can help them produce bigger results.

This is what I've focused my life on, and I can now accomplish in a single conversation what would have taken me a whole year of coaching to do 20 years ago.

Who wouldn't want a life focused on an activity that's fascinating and motivating, that involves making your best possible contribution, and that's appreciated by those most important to you?

The Strategic Coach Program
For Game-Changing Entrepreneurs

You commit to growing upward through three game-changing levels, giving yourself 25 years to transform every aspect of your work and life.

A lot of people might think they want to be a Game Changer, but they hope it will just happen for them. The Strategic Coach Program—a quarterly workshop experience for successful entrepreneurs—is for those who are committed and devoted to business and industry transformation for the long-term, for 25 years and beyond.

For many of them, this starts long before they're actually in business. They have an instinct about themselves and how they want to create their future that likely started in childhood. They've fought for their ability to control their time, to control how their money is made, to work with those they want to work with both inside their business and out in the marketplace, and there's a real purpose to their life, with the result that being buried inside of someone else's system could never be satisfactory.

If you've reached a jumping off point in your entrepreneurial career where you're beyond ready to multiply all of your capabilities and opportunities into a 10x more creative and productive formula that keeps getting simpler and more satisfying, we're ready for you.

Being a hero.

The idea of being a hero is integral to understanding the fundamental and underlying concept of The Strategic Coach Program, WhoNotHow, which is all about freeing yourself up to be a hero. It involves asking yourself the right question when you come up with a new idea.

Instead of asking yourself, *"How* can I do this?" ask, *"Who* can do this?" This simple question prevents procrastination and ensures the right people (the "Whos") with the right skills are doing all the necessary "Hows" to bring your ideas to life.

This way of operating keeps you focused on what you love to do and do best and ensures you're freed up to create value for others using your unique capabilities and skills.

Three game-changing levels.

Strategic Coach participants continually transform how they think, make decisions, communicate, and take action based on their use of dozens of unique entrepreneurial mindsets we've developed. The Program has been refined through decades of entrepreneurial testing and is the most concentrated, massive discovery process in the world created solely for entrepreneurs who want to change their game.

Over the years, we've observed that our clients' development happens in levels of mastery. And so, we've organized the Program into three levels of participation, each of which involves two different ways of changing your game:

The Signature Level. The first level is devoted to coming to grips with your *personal game*, which has to do with how you're spending your time as an entrepreneur as well as how you're taking advantage of your personal freedom outside of business that your entrepreneurial success affords you. Upping your personal game before you move on to making significant changes in other aspects of your life and business is key because you have to simplify before you can multiply.

The second aspect of this level is how you look at your *teamwork game*. This means seeing that your future consists of teamwork with others whose unique capabilities complement your own, leading to bigger and better goals that constantly get achieved at a measurably higher rate.

The 10x Ambition Level. Once you feel confident about your own personal game and have access to ever-expanding teamwork, you can think much bigger in terms of your *company game*. An idea that at one time would have seemed scary and even impossible—growing your business 10x—is no longer a wild dream but a result of the systematic expansion of the teamwork model you've established. And because you're stable in the center, you won't get thrown off balance by exponential growth. Your life stays balanced and integrated even as things grow around you.

And that's when you're in a position to change your *market game*. This is when your company has a huge impact on the marketplace that competitors can't even understand. This is because they're not going through this game-changing structure or thinking in terms of 25 years as you are. Thinking in terms of 25 years gives you an expansive sense of freedom, while focusing on 90 days at a time within that framework gives you a remarkable sense of focus.

The Game Changer Level. Once you've mastered the first four types of "games," you're at the point where your company is self-managing and self-multiplying, which means that your time can now be totally freed up. At this stage, competitors become collaborators and it becomes an *industry game*. You can consider everything you've created as a single capability you can now match up with another company's to create collaborations that go way beyond 10x.

And, finally, it becomes a *global game*. You immediately see that there are possibilities of going global—it's just a matter of combining your capabilities with those of others to create something exponentially bigger than you could ever have achieved on your own.

36 mind-shifting core concepts.

With these three growth levels, there's a continual upward mastery of 36 mind-shifting concepts. These core concepts continually integrate with one another and evolve. Dozens more innovative concepts exist in the Program that support these core concepts.

Global game-changing community.

Entrepreneurism can be a lonely activity. You have goals that the people you grew up with don't understand. Your family might not comprehend you at all and don't know why you keep wanting to expand, why you want to take new risks, why you want to jump to the next level. And so it becomes proportionately more important as you gain your own individual mastery that you're in a community of thousands of individuals who are on exactly the same journey.

In The Strategic Coach Program, you benefit from not only your own continual individual mastery but from the constant expansion of support from and collaboration with a growing global community of extraordinarily liberated entrepreneurs who will increasingly share with you their deep wisdom and creative breakthroughs as Game Changers in hundreds of different industries and markets.

For more information and to register for The Strategic Coach Program, call 416.531.7399 or 1.800.387.3206, or visit us online at *strategiccoach.com*.

ENTREPRENEURS

GAME CHANGER

25	26	27	28
29	30	31	32
33	34	35	36

10X AMBITION

13	14	15	16
17	18	19	20
21	22	23	24

SIGNATURE

1	2	3	4
5	6	7	8
9	10	11	12

WHO

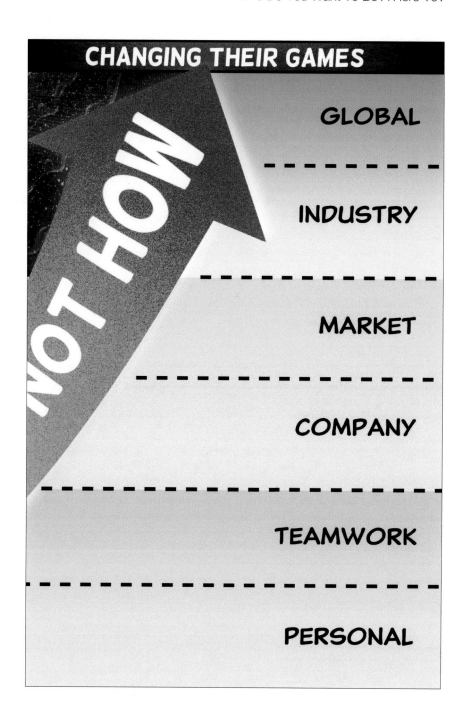

The "Who Do You Want To Be A Hero To?" Scorecard

Turn the page to view the Mindset Scorecard and read through the four statements for each mindset. Give yourself a score of 1 to 12 based on where your own mindset falls on the spectrum. Put each mindset's score in the first column at the right, and then add up all eight and put the total at the bottom.

Then, think about what scores would represent progress for you over the next quarter. Write these in the second scoring column, add them up, and write in the total.

When you compare the two scores, you can see where you want to go in terms of your achievements and ambitions.

Mindsets	1	2	3	4	5	6
1 Being A Hero Is About Them	You've always experienced yourself as an isolated individual and as a failure because no one appreciates anything you think or do.			You're increasingly aware that life isn't all about you and that being more successful requires being more useful to others.		
2 It's About *Their* Bigger Future	You increasingly resent other people's progress because you feel that their success is always the result of having unfair advantages.			You're just now realizing that being more useful to others speeds up your own advancement, and you feel that you have to make up for lost time.		
3 Transforming Their D.O.S.	You're always so distracted by what's not working in your own daily life that you can't think about anyone else's experience.			You're increasingly aware and anxious that what people will need and want in the future goes way beyond what you're trying to provide.		
4 They Grow, You Expand	Your unhappiness with your own situation keeps getting worse because it seems that other people are only thinking about themselves.			You're coming to the painful realization that competing over scarce opportunities is undermining your ability to learn and improve.		
5 Your Crucial Contribution	You've never seen that what you want and need has anything to do with what other people want and need — except that they don't care.			You feel frustrated that none of your conventional education and training has clarified how you can be uniquely useful and rewarded in the future.		
6 Easy To Commit For 25 Years	You're so bogged down and pulled backward by your past failures that you can't even visualize what a better tomorrow would look like.			You feel that there has to be a better way of creating your future life than just reacting to outside changes and pressures.		
7 Heroes Attract Each Other	Your experience of relating to other people is so chronically disappointing that you can't see how you can trust anyone in the future.			You realize that being crucially important in ways you enjoy now requires that you significantly transform how you're operating.		
8 Exponential Hero Networks	You're becoming increasingly isolated and sorry for yourself because you can see that everyone else is feeling exactly the same way.			You have an urgent need to separate yourself from everything stagnant in your life and begin transforming yourself in entirely new ways.		
Scorecard	➡	➡	➡	➡	➡	➡ ➡ ➡

7	8	9	10	11	12	Score Now	Score Next
You've worked hard all your life to perform and achieve in a way that demonstrates that you're more successful than other people.			You're amazed at how being a hero to someone else always expands your awareness, capabilities, and value outward into the world.				
You're always conscious of how your status in life — including your professional reputation and quality of lifestyle — compares with others.			You gain great clarity and confidence from knowing that enabling other people's improvement and growth uniquely accelerates your own.				
You've learned everything you'll ever need to know about other people's needs in order to be successful in selling your products and services.			You're certain that being a hero starts by first understanding other individuals' biggest dangers, opportunities, and strengths.				
You always make sure that your successes and achievements are superior to those of everyone else you work and live with.			Your hero confidence continually increases because the more you help others grow, the more your capabilities to be a hero expand.				
You've mastered knowledge and skills that your training and experience tell you will always be required by other successful people in the years ahead.			You increasingly use your best capabilities to uniquely help certain individuals achieve goals that are crucial to their future growth.				
You know that your present formula for working and living successfully sets you up for the rest of your career and your retirement years.			You're increasingly relaxed by the growing certainty that being a unique hero in other people's futures can keep growing over the next 25 years.				
You've arranged all of your personal and business relationships so that no one can ever fail or disappoint you in a serious way.			You find that as you master being a crucial hero in others' lives, you also attract other heroes who will be creative collaborators with you.				
You've accepted that you're simply who you are and that it's not likely that anything important is going to change from now on.			You realize that the more you grow as a hero to certain individuals, the more you automatically connect with others who are doing the same.				
➡ ➡ ➡ ➡			➡ ➡ ➡ ➡				

About The Author
Dan Sullivan

Dan Sullivan is the founder and president of The Strategic Coach Inc. and creator of The Strategic Coach® Program, which helps accomplished entrepreneurs reach new heights of success and happiness.

He has over 40 years of experience as a strategic planner and coach to entrepreneurial individuals and groups. He is author of over 30 publications, including *The 80% Approach*™, *The Dan Sullivan Question*, *Ambition Scorecard*, *Wanting What You Want*, *The 4 C's Formula*, *The 25-Year Framework*, *The Game Changer*, *The 10x Mind Expander*, *The Mindset Scorecard*, *The Self-Managing Company*, *Procrastination Priority*, *The Gap And The Gain*, *The ABC Breakthrough*, *Extraordinary Impact Filter*, *Capableism*, *My Plan For Living To 156*, *WhoNotHow*, and *Your Life As A Strategy Circle*, and is co-author with Catherine Nomura of *The Laws of Lifetime Growth*.

Made in the USA
San Bernardino, CA
10 January 2020